ALICE AND MARTIN PROVENSEN
Our Animal Friends

AT MAPLE HILL FARM

A RANDOM HOUSE BOOK

Copyright © 1974 by Alice and Martin Provensen. All rights reserved under International and Pan-American Copyright Conventions. Published in the United States by Random House, Inc., New York, and simultaneously in Canada by Random House of Canada Limited, Toronto.
Library of Congress Cataloging in Publication Data.
Provensen, Alice   Our animal friends at Maple Hill farm.   Describes animals on the authors' own farm in New York: dogs, horses, pigs, geese, chickens, cows, goats, sheep, cats, and more! [1. Animals—Fiction.   2. Farm life—Fiction]   I. Provensen, Martin, joint author. II. Title.   PZ10.3.P928Ap   [E]   74-828   ISBN 0-394-82123-8   ISBN 0-394-92123-2 (lib. bdg.)
Manufactured in the United States of America
1 2 3 4 5 6 7 8 9 0

WHO LIVES AT MAPLE HILL FARM?

People live here.
Two dogs and five horses live here.
A pig lives here.
Then there are—
        some geese,
        lots of chickens,
        a few cows,
        a few goats,
        several sheep,
        and four special cats.

CAT NAP

Here are the four cats curled up together.

The four special cats sleep together in the chimney corner, where it is warm. When they are awake it is easier to tell them apart.

EGGNOG is a Siamese cat.
She is very, very old and
she is never warm enough.

Eggnog has a sweet nature,
though she throws up a lot
and hates to go out-of-doors.

She is cross-eyed and
has a lumpy tail.

WILLOW is Eggnog's niece.
Her father's name was
Potato Who Disappeared.

Willow has beautiful eyes
and an elegant tail,
but she is not interesting.

She doesn't like to play.
She doesn't like to fight.

GOOSEBERRY was named for the color of her eyes.
She was a playful stray kitten who grew up
to be a good gray cat.
Now she has kittens of her own
to play with.

And then there is...

MAX

MAX is Gooseberry's son. Max is BIG.
He is still very young. He has a tiny, high voice
and he likes cottage cheese.

Max and Gooseberry are always spitting at each other,
as you will see, but Max likes children and he likes to play.

Max can be scratchy.
You have to be careful when you play with him.
He is not very clever with his claws.

Max is clever enough to catch
mice and rabbits and squirrels.
It is not a pretty sight.

He leaves gifts of guts and tails
and chipmunk heads on the doorstep.
Not a pretty sight either.

But, then, no cats are vegetarians.
It's not in their nature.

Gooseberry and Max are
spitting at each other.

Eggnog is using
the cat pan.

Max
is teasing
a chipmunk.
It's not a pretty sight.

Gooseberry is nursing her kittens.
She is a good mother to them.

Max is pretending to be
asleep. He won't hurt
the hen. She is too big.

Willow is not
interested in
chickens.

Max hates snakes.

Gooseberry is washing a kitten.

Max is hiding in the garden.

Eggnog is exploring
a brown paper bag.

Willow is
sitting still.

Gooseberry is moving a kitten
from one place to another.

Eggnog is eating
an umbrella plant.

Willow is not interested
in umbrella plants.

Gooseberry is moving a kitten
from one place to another.

Gooseberry and Max are
spitting at each other.

Willow is washing,
though she is never dirty.

Eggnog is looking
out the window.

Willow is sitting still.

Max is watching a bird.

Gooseberry is drinking milk.

Max is tangling
with a ball of yarn.

Eggnog is using
the cat pan.

Willow is very beautiful, but
she is not very interesting.

THE CHICKENS are interesting. There are hens who lay eg

This nice big brown
chicken is called
GOOD OLD LITTLE RED HEN.
There are many more brown
hens like her.

There is only one
polka-dot hen.
She is named
OTHER HEN.

This little
black hen is
called SWEETY.
There are many more
black hens like her.

Here is a brown egg.

Here is a white egg.

Both eggs are good.

d there are roosters who have long tails and crow.

This rooster
is named
LOVELACE.

This
rooster
is named
POLA
NEGRI.

This big rooster
is named BIG SHOT.
He doesn't like
children.

Big Shot is fighting
with Pola Negri.

Sweety lays brown
eggs, but she doesn't
like to sit on them.

Other Hen lays white
eggs. She doesn't like
to sit on eggs either.

Good Old Little Red Hen
is too old to lay eggs,
but she loves to sit
on other hens' eggs.

Pola Negri has found
a good pink worm.
All the hens come
running to share it.

Big Shot is fighting with Lovelace.

Other Hen is taking a dust bath.

Good Old Little Red Hen
is asleep on a nest of eggs.

All the other chickens are asleep
in the chicken coop.

All but Big Shot, who
sleeps in the trees.

Sweety and Other Hen
are taking a sun bath.

Good Old Little Red Hen
is sitting on eggs.

Lovelace has scratched up
a batch of good ants.
All the hens come running
to share them.

Big Shot won't let
the hens have any corn.

Big Shot is picking
on Sweety.

A fox
is carrying
Big Shot away.

Good Old Little Red Hen has ten baby chicks.
She is a good mother to them.

Lovelace
and
Pola Negri
are crowing.

DOGGEREL

Here are the two dogs
who live on the farm.
They are very special dogs.

MUFFIN is nine months old.
She is big for her age and may grow even bigger.
Now she weighs 41 pounds.

Muffin has many pet names.
Sometimes she is called Raga Muffin;
sometimes Mafia,
other times—Beasty, Gorilla or Fiend.

No one knows what kind of dog she is.

DINAH is thirteen years old.
Dinah is small for her age,
but no one expected her to
grow any larger.
She is that kind of dog.
She stopped growing
long ago.

Dinah has nicknames too.
Hers are: Dine
          Diner
          Nosy Parker
          and
          Little Sister.

HOW TO WEIGH A DOG

$$\begin{array}{r} 91 \\ -50 \\ \hline 41 \end{array}$$

Muffin weighs
41 pounds.

Hold the dog in your arms.
Step on the scale.
See how much you weigh together.

Let the dog go.
Step on the scale.
See how much you weigh alone.

Subtract the small number from the large number. The answer is what the dog weighs.

How much does
Dinah weigh?

Cats can be weighed this way, too.
So can a horse if your scale is strong enough and you can lift a horse.

Dinah is crazy about STONES. She carries stones from one place to another.

It is hard to understand how she can carry them since she has so few teeth left.

Dinah doesn't like anyone to see where she puts the stones. Perhaps she is building something. She is doing her work.

Muffin doesn't do any work. She picks up big sticks, hoping to tempt someone to play with her.

Dogs like to play.

DOG GAMES

Both Dinah and Muffin like to play ball—
but they don't play the same way.

When you throw
a ball for them,
Dinah finds it
by smelling
where it went.
Muffin has to see
where it went.

If Dinah gets the ball
first, she brings it
back, hoping you will
throw it again.

If Muffin gets the ball,
she runs away with it,
hoping you will chase her.

When there's no one to play with, dogs are sometimes bored.

When Dinah is bored, she curls up and goes to sleep.

When Muffin is bored, she chews up pillows...

barks at geese...

teases Max...

and chases horses—a very dangerous game.

HORSEPLAY

IBN RAFFERTY
is chasing Ichabod.

CHAOS
is chasing Ichabod.

They don't mean
anything
by it.
It's just that
everybody chases
ICHABOD.

Everybody except COMANCHE, who likes Ichabod, and LUCKY,
who is fat, lazy, and good-natured and thinks only about eating.

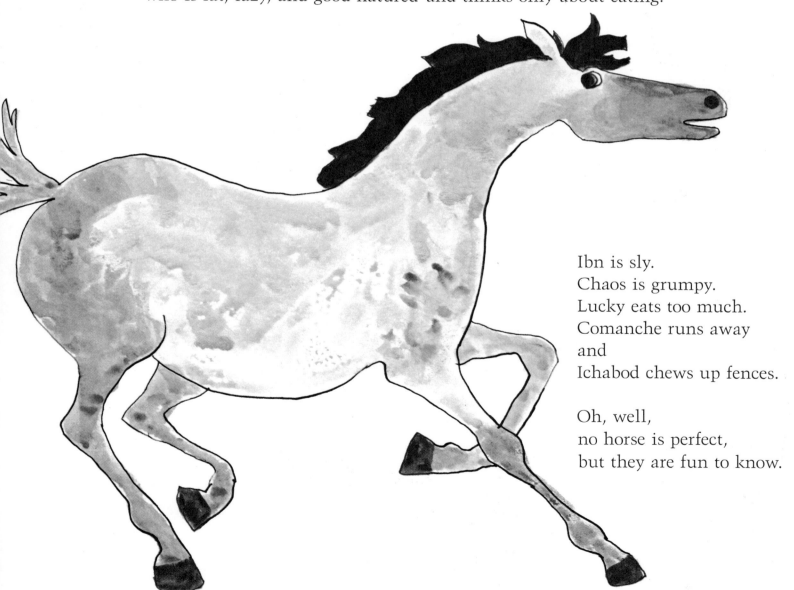

Ibn is sly.
Chaos is grumpy.
Lucky eats too much.
Comanche runs away
and
Ichabod chews up fences.

Oh, well,
no horse is perfect,
but they are fun to know.

IBN RAFFERTY is called a gray, but really he is a white horse.
Ibn's nickname is Big White Pill.

Ibn is almost impossible to catch, and you can *never* catch him by running after him.

If you stand very quietly and for a long while, Ibn will come to you and let you put a bridle on him. He teaches you to be patient, but sometimes you can't help wishing he were different.

Once Ibn stepped
on a nail and had
to keep his foot wrapped
in hot bandages,
inside a big plastic bag
with a gunny sack
tied around.
He was very quiet
and friendly then.
He knew he
had been hurt.

After Ibn has been
brushed
and
combed
and
curried—
and
looks clean
and
beautiful—
he rolls in the mud.

It is very funny
to see a horse rolling.
It makes you laugh
even though
all your work
has been wasted.

The good thing
about Ibn is that
he is fun to ride.
He never plays any tricks
when he is out for a ride.

CHAOS is crazy about LUCKY.

Chaos is old now and cranky, but he will still jump a fence in the spring,
when he is feeling cheerful and spry. The best thing about Chaos is that he likes
people. He doesn't mind if people come close. He is easy to catch.
Lucky is crazy about carrots and corn and sugar and apples and children.
She lets children comb her and brush her and pick up her feet.

Lucky lets children walk
around her and under her.
She lets them
sit on her.
Lucky stands very quietly
when children are near.

Hold your hand flat
when you feed a pony,
or the pony may
pinch your fingers
by mistake.

It is best to wear shoes when
you are around a horse or a pony.
They would hurt your bare toes
if they happened to step on them.

Lucky loves to swim in the pond. You can go with her if you know how
to swim, too, and don't mind getting your clothes wet.
Lucky will take you for a ride, but when she gets tired she lets you know it.
She will roll over. Be quick and get out of the way or she will roll on you
and she weighs 600 pounds! Lucky is a small pony but she is fat.

But then,
no pony is perfect.

ICHABOD and COMANCHE
are very sure-footed
and they love to gallop.
Though horses are big, they are shy and easily frightened.
You have to be careful to hang on.
They are afraid of silly little things like unexpected pieces of paper.
And sometimes they want their own way and take you home before you are ready to go.

Everybody loves horses, except some people who are afraid of them.

Oh, well,
no people
are perfect.

THE GEESE are nearly perfect—
at least they act that way.

They are strong and healthy.
They never catch cold,
and they live to be a hundred.

Geese eat
grass and weeds
and hay
and corn

and almost
anything else
that is good
to eat.

Geese have
wonderful
eyesight.
They can see
a bird
or
a plane
a half-mile
away.

This goose is a gander.
His name is EVIL MURDOCH.

Geese have keen ears.
They can hear the family car
on its way home, and they
gabble to greet it.

Geese
like
horses.

Because they
are so noisy,
geese make
good watchdogs.
They
can even
scare a fox away.

Geese are
good swimmers
and
good mothers
and fathers.

The only trouble
with geese is...

GEESE have bad tempers.

They are greedy.
They are grabby.
They are grouchy.

They grumble.
They gabble.
They grinch.
They grunch
and
they grabble.

AND THEY PINCH.

Farm geese can't fly.
When they see the wild geese migrating,
they start to walk after them
and have to be brought home again.

Then they bully the dogs,
complain to the cats,
and pinch the sheep's heels.

That's the trouble with geese,
who otherwise are nearly perfect.

THE SHEEP are silly. They are so silly the geese can hardly be blamed for wantin

This sheep has a black face. This sheep has a white face. This sheep has a whit
Almost all sheep's wool is supposed to be white. Most of the time their woc
Almost all sheep look very much alike and do very much the same thing

Sheep eat together.

Sheep sleep together.

o pinch them. Still, there's something sweet about sheep even if they aren't clever.

ace and horns. They are all ewes. This sheep has a white face and horns and is a ram.
s gray and full of thistles and burrs and straw and mud and dirt and flowers.
nd they do the same things at the same time and all together.

When they are lost, sheep bleat together.   All but one . . .

OLD ELEVEN doesn't really need an earring for you to tell her
from the other sheep. She is smarter.

Old Eleven
can always find
her way home and
the other sheep follow her.
She always knows where
the gate is, and the other sheep
follow her through it.

Old Eleven
is the best sheep,
and the best thing
about her is that
in the spring, when
she has lambs, she
always has twin lambs.

The best thing about sheep is TWIN BABY LAMBS.

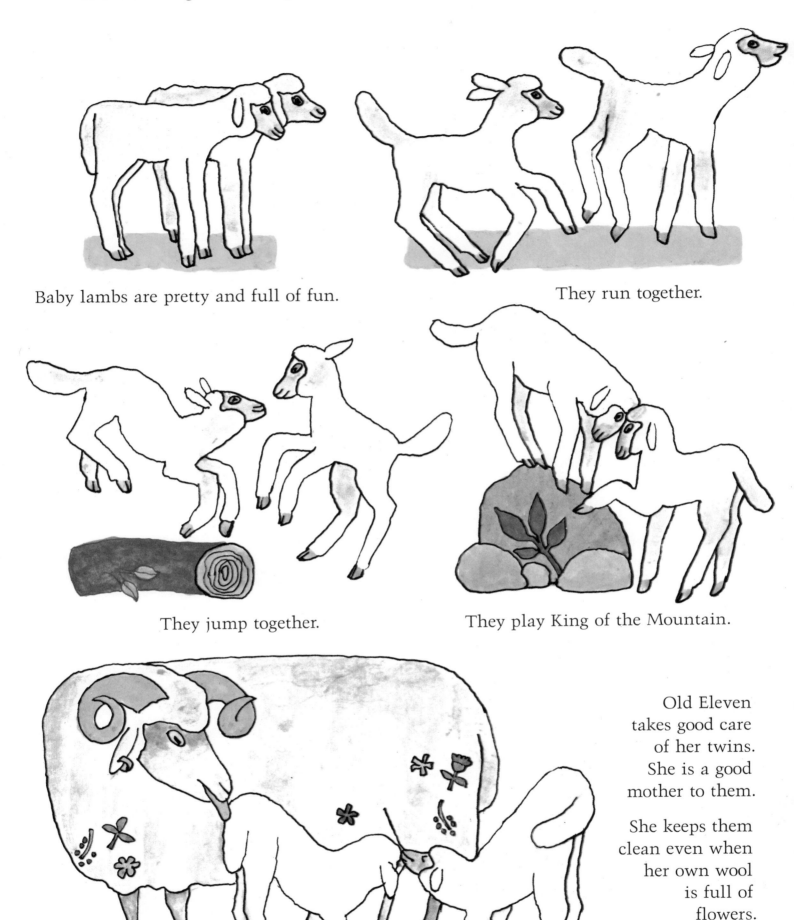

Baby lambs are pretty and full of fun.

They run together.

They jump together.

They play King of the Mountain.

Old Eleven takes good care of her twins. She is a good mother to them.

She keeps them clean even when her own wool is full of flowers.

The only trouble with baby lambs is they grow so quickly and become sheep.

WHINEY is one of the twin lambs who has grown up.
She didn't inherit any of her mother's brains.

She is always lost and
never knows where the gate is.

Whiney is never sure where her own lambs are.
This confuses her and makes her cry.

She can't tell a good blade of grass
from a poison weed, so she is often sick.

She faints
from fear when her wool is being shorn.

But Whiney has a good friend who likes her and looks after her—

a BILLY GOAT named SAM.

Sam is not afraid
of anything.
He knows how to
stand and face
a dog or a goose
who tries to tease him.
Because Sam doesn't
run away,
they always stop
teasing.

Sam can pull a cart full of children—

when he wants to!

Once in a while Sam gets tired of being in his field and butts his way out.

This makes everyone angry. Not only does the fence have to be repaired, but when Sam is free he eats the roses.

Thorns and all!

NANNY GOATS are just as clever as billy goats, but they are not nearly so cranky. They have beards, too.

GOAT DEAR is a white goat.
She is very gentle and likes people.

M-A-A-A
is brown.

Whiney likes M-a-a-a
and Goat Dear, too.

Goat Dear gives you her milk
except when she has kids of her own.

Goat Dear likes kids and children.
She seems to smile at them.

Kids are lively
and full of
fun.

They run together.   They jump together.   They play King of the Mountain, too.

KIDS don't have to butt their way out of fields.

They can jump over almost any fence, out of any field, and into any garden.

Kids love gardens. SISTER is eating the green beans. BROTHER likes cabbage.

When they are chased out of the garden, they start pulling down the clothes.

Kids are clever and full of fun but, oh, they can be a terrible nuisance!

THE COWS don't like to be fenced in either.
They don't jump out or butt out. They lean out.

Cows are strong and stubborn. They lean their way right through a barbed-wire fence—barbs and all. This makes everyone angry. The fence has to be repaired.

When the cows are loose, they wander heavily in all directions, always in a hurry. They trample the corn in the fields. They trample the vegetables in the garden.

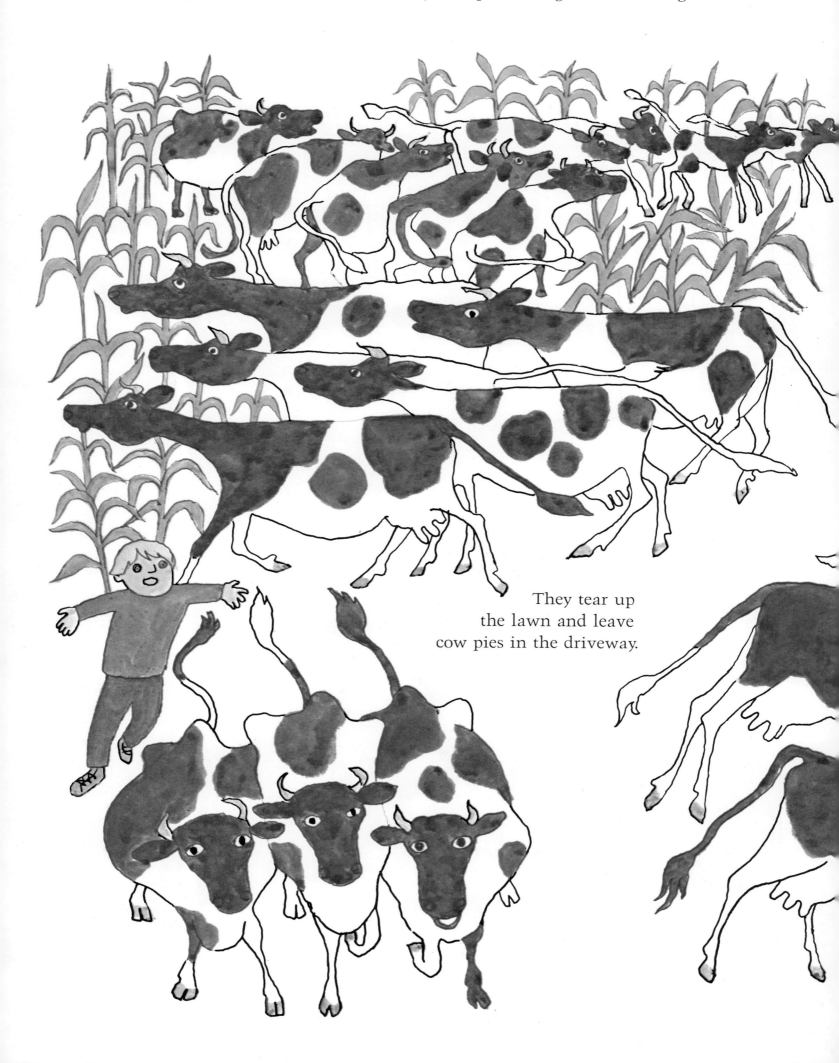

They tear up the lawn and leave cow pies in the driveway.

Cows are very valuable but they can be a nuisance, too.
They cause the neighbors to call up and complain.

GOOD NEIGHBORS are valuable and well-loved.
These dogs are good neighbors.
They do valuable things.

This dog is a good watchdog.
His name is LOTHAR.

This dog is a good companion.
Her name is DUTCHESS.

This dog is a good playmate.
His name is EL PUPPO.

This dog is a good mother dog.
Her name is POPPY.

Other dogs are foolish dogs who do useless, foolish things.
These dogs aren't around any more.

This dog
bit people.
Now she lives
in a kennel.
Her name is
BISCUIT.

This dog chased cars and was run over.
His name was CANNY.

This dog killed sheep and had to be put away (as the saying goes). His name was ARGOS.

This dog snapped at children
and wet on beds.
He is not around any more either.
His name was SWEENEY.

This dog ran away from home
and went to live with
someone else.
No one can remember his name.

PIGS only look foolish. They have funny eyes and crazy tails, but they are said to be the cleverest of all animals.
Pigs are sometimes hogs.
They are always
hungry.

Here is a piglet named PEARL.
Pearl was raised in
an old playpen.
She grew up
quickly.

Now Pearl lives in a pigpen and has piglets of her own to feed.
She is a good mother to them.

OTHER NEIGHBORS
live in the swamps and fields
of the farm on Maple Hill.
It is not easy to get to know them,
but they let themselves be seen now and then.
You can tell when they have paid a visit.
They get hungry, too.

A RACCOON comes at night and takes his share
of the harvest corn, which is probably only fair.

Some neighbors would be
loved better somewhere
else. WOODCHUCKS dig
big holes in the pastures.
They hurry into them
when the dogs are around.

VOLES tunnel in the
grass and MOLES tunnel
in holes. The cats
can catch them because
cats are patient and
wait for them to come out.

CHIPMUNKS hide
in the stone walls.
They are peaceful
little creatures,
but the cats wait for
them to come out, too.

A SKUNK is walking by. Skunks don't hurry
or hide. The dogs and cats pretend not
to notice them. It is best not to.

All sorts of bugs and beetles
and bees live around the farm—
especially WASPS.

BIRDS visit the bird feeder in the wintertime. GRAY SQUIRRELS come there, too. Squirrels love bird feed.

RED SQUIRRELS store things in the attic. They drop nuts down between the walls at night, keeping everyone awake.

FROGS and FISH and TURTLES live in the pond. A MUSKRAT lives there, too.

A TOAD with golden eyes lives near the pump.

He never hides either. No one bothers toads. They taste terrible.

MOTHS hang around the outside light at night.

A POSSUM is another night neighbor. He rattles the dog pans, looking for left-over leftovers.

MORE NEIGHBORS live close by.

FIELD MICE are on the pantry shelves.
Why don't they stay in the fields?

A SPIDER is spinning
a web in the basement.

An old LAND TORTOISE is moving his
house to another part of the land.

ANTS live in an ant hill in the pasture.
Sometimes they visit the garbage can.

A MOTHER SKUNK is walking by with her babies. Please do not notice her.

WORMS live in the apples.

A GRASS SNAKE
lives in the grass.

RABBITS are interested in the garden.
You must plant enough lettuce for the
neighbors. That is, if you like salad.

A HAWK flies over the barnyard in
the wintertime. He is looking for
someone to eat. He is hungry too.

WOODPECKERS are
pecking on the
mailbox post.

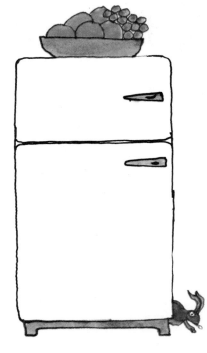

A CRICKET is
wintering in back
of the refrigerator.

No one has ever seen the PORCUPINE, but he lives here all right. He leaves footprints in the snow.

IN A QUIET CORNER of an overgrown field,
where the snow lies deepest and the oak trees hold their leaves all winter,
a beloved hound, named John, lies buried.
Three cats are buried here—Webster, the first Siamese,
a dear, dirty white cat named Crook, who stole from the table,
and Fat Boy, who looked like Max.

In this quiet corner, the best wild flowers grow,
and the first peepers are heard in the spring, even before the snow melts.
Here, owls call from the treetops in the early morning,
and the irreverent crows hold their noisy conventions.
Here, the mother deer has her fawn, and the migrating geese come to rest.
It is here that the fox is safe from the hunters.

The animals that were...

the animals that are...

and the animals that will be...

bring joy, laughter, and life to the lives of the people who live in a house

...hat needs painting, at the end of a road full of holes.... MAPLE HILL FARM.